Birding in Lisbon

Gonçalo Elias

Birding in Lisbon

Title: Birding in Lisbon
Author (text and maps): Gonçalo Elias
Cover page: Firecrest *Regulus ignicapilla* (Pedro Marques)
Digital illustrations: C. Maria Elias
Production: C. Maria Elias
Printing: Createspace.com
Distribution: Amazon.com

1st edition, August 2017

ISBN: 978-1973881087

Print On Demand

Contact: goncalo.elias@gmail.com

CONTENTS

Where is Lisbon

Lisbon is Portugal's largest city and capital. It lies on the west coast, on the right side of the river Tagus. The municipality (concelho) of Lisbon covers an area of 100 km². It is bordered to the south and east by the river Tagus, to the north by the municipalities of Loures and Odivelas and to the west by the municipalities of Amadora and Oeiras.

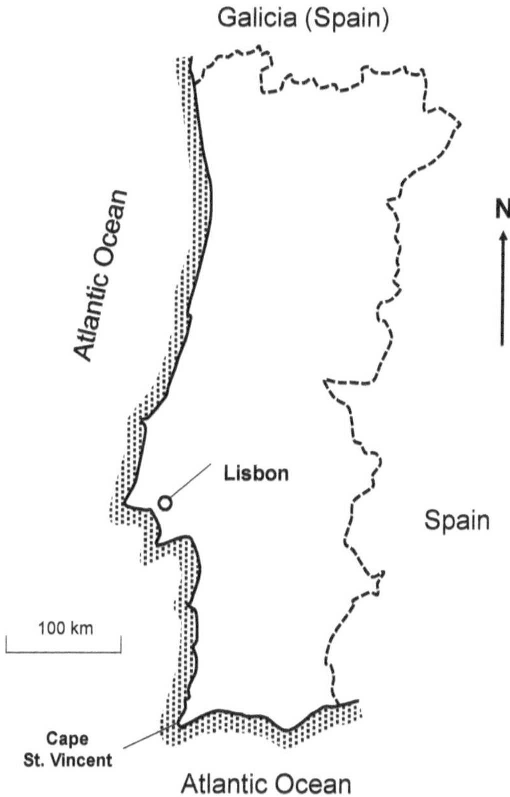

Map of Portugal showing the location of Lisbon, the country's capital

Birding in Lisbon

Lisbon offers many birdwatching opportunities.

The city lies on the right side of the river Tagus, close to the estuary. This estuary is the largest in the country and attracts a lot of waterbirds, especially outside the breeding season. Some areas of estuarine muds lie close to the city and this means that it is possible to see a good selection of waterbirds, especially during low tide.

Additionally, as is the case with most large cities, there are several parks and gardens. Many of these are also suitable for birdwatching.

In this booklet we present a number of birding hotspots in Lisbon, aiming at helping anyone with an interest in birds to get the best birding opportunities.

Hotspot selection has been made taking into account bird variety and ease of access.

A short description is provided for each hotspot, along with a list of the most interesting birds to be found there and some suggestions of how it can be explored.

Nine hotspots have been selected. Three of them are located near the river, while the remaining ones are scattered throughout the city (please see map on the following page).

The riverine hotspots are as follows:

- Belém (3) – in the western part of the city, close to several famous monuments
- Matinha (8) – lies in the eastern part of Lisbon harbour
- Parque do Tejo (9) – at the north-eastern tip of the town, with a good view over the estuary

As to the parks and gardens, the following ones are recommended:

- Monsanto (1) – this is the largest park in town
- Tapada da Ajuda (2) – an enclosed area at the southern tip of Monsanto

- Parque Bensaúde (4) – a small park in the Benfica area, noted for its three species of parrots
- Jardim Calouste Gulbenkian (5) – a small park with a lake in the central part of the city
- Quinta das Conchas (6) – a medium-sized park in northern Lisbon, not far from the airport
- Parque da Bela Vista (7) – an open area on top of a hill

All places in this book can easily be reached using public transport. More details about this option are provided at the end of the book.

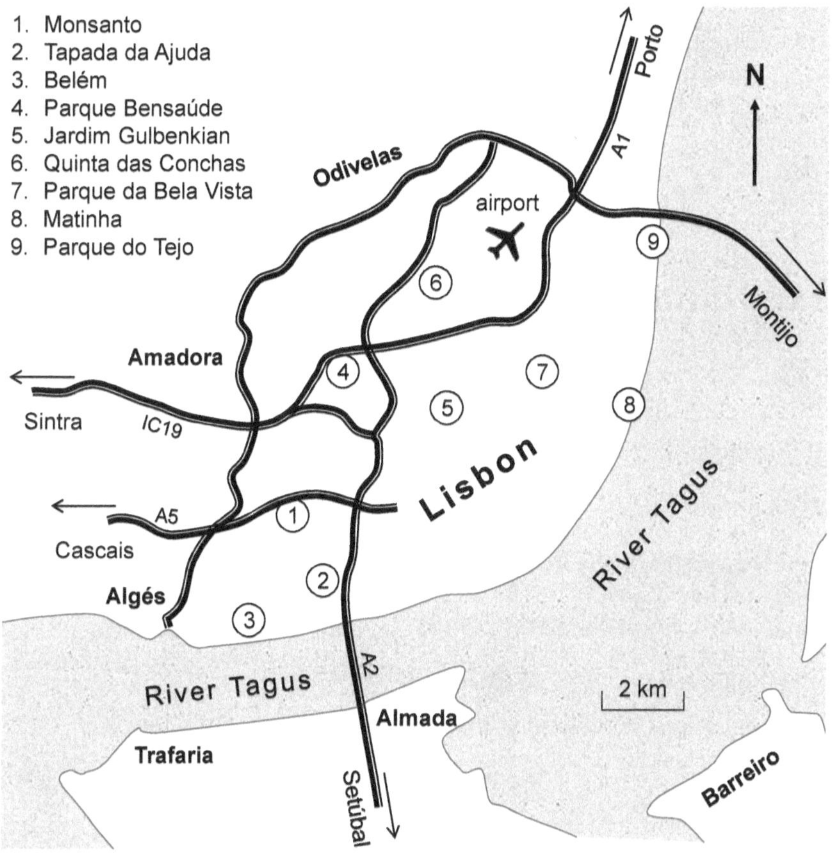

Map of birding hotspots in Lisbon

Monsanto

This is Lisbon's largest park – it lies just west of the city. Although a motorway (A5) runs through it, some areas are for pedestrians only and provide good birdwatching opportunities.

Birds

Resident: Red-legged Partridge, Night Heron, Buzzard, Great Spotted Woodpecker, Grey Wagtail, Sardinian Warbler, Firecrest, Long-tailed Tit, Coal Tit, Short-toed Treecreeper, Jay, Spotless Starling, Serin

Breeding visitors: Turtle Dove, Swift, Pallid Swift

Non-breeding visitors: Meadow Pipit, Song Thrush, Chiffchaff, Pied Flycatcher, Siskin

How to visit it

This area is best reached by car, either from the south (Alcântara), from the east (Amoreiras) or from the north (Benfica). Free parking is available at many locations.

There are several places worth visiting. For convenience, we will consider two different sub-areas: south and north of the A5 motorway.

South of the A5, the best spots are Montes Claros (A) and Alameda Keil do Amaral (B). At Montes Claros, there is a small lake with feral ducks; Grey Wagtail is often around and Night Heron turns up here at times. In the surrounding trees there are usually Coal and Long-tailed Tits, as well as Firecrest.

Alameda Keil do Amaral lies slightly to the northeast of Montes Claros; it is a walking area that comprises woodland and a few clearings. This place has a network of trails, where it is possible to bird quietly. Species here include Black Redstart, Sardinian Warbler, Short-toed Treecreeper and Firecrest.

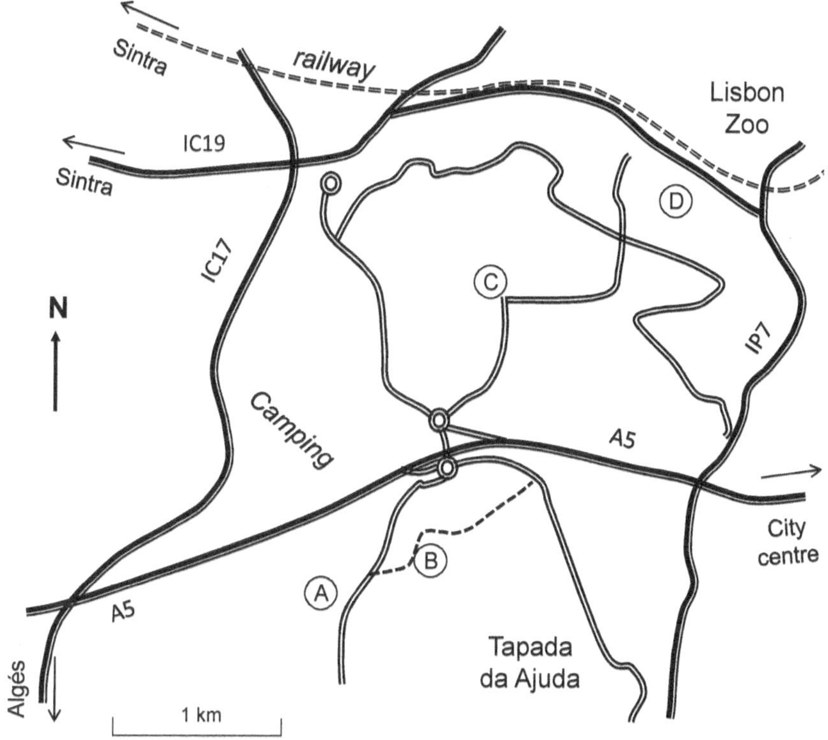

The area north of the A5 is larger, but the birding places may be a little more difficult to find. Just in the centre of this sector lies Forte de Monsanto (C), currently used as a prison. Just south of it there are some open fields, which hold Zitting Cisticola and sometimes Stonechat. In winter there are often a few Meadow Pipits.

To the east of Forte de Monsanto lies Parque do Calhau (D) – this area, which can also be reached on foot from Sete Rios (close to the zoo) has the largest patch of cork oaks in town.

Tapada da Ajuda

A large park at the southern end of Monsanto. The whole area is enclosed by a wall and traffic is limited. It is well wooded, but there are also a few open fields.

Birds

Resident: Red-legged Partridge, Buzzard, Ring-necked Parakeet, Great Spotted Woodpecker, Black Redstart, Zitting Cisticola, Sardinian Warbler, Firecrest, Coal Tit, Short-toed Treecreeper, Jay, Serin, Common Waxbill

Breeding visitors: Turtle Dove, Common Swift, Pallid Swift

Non-breeding visitors: Meadow Pipit, Song Thrush, Chiffchaff, Spotted Flycatcher, Pied Flycatcher, Chaffinch, Linnet

How to visit it

The main entrance lies on the south side, near Rua Jau. Drivers can only enter with permission or by paying a small fee. Alternatively, it is possible to park outside and enter on foot, as pedestrians can enter free of charge. Visitors might be asked for identification at the gate, although this is not always the case. The Tapada is formed by a network of roads and tracks. Car movement is largely concentrated on the southern half, so it is better to get to the northern part, which is much quieter.

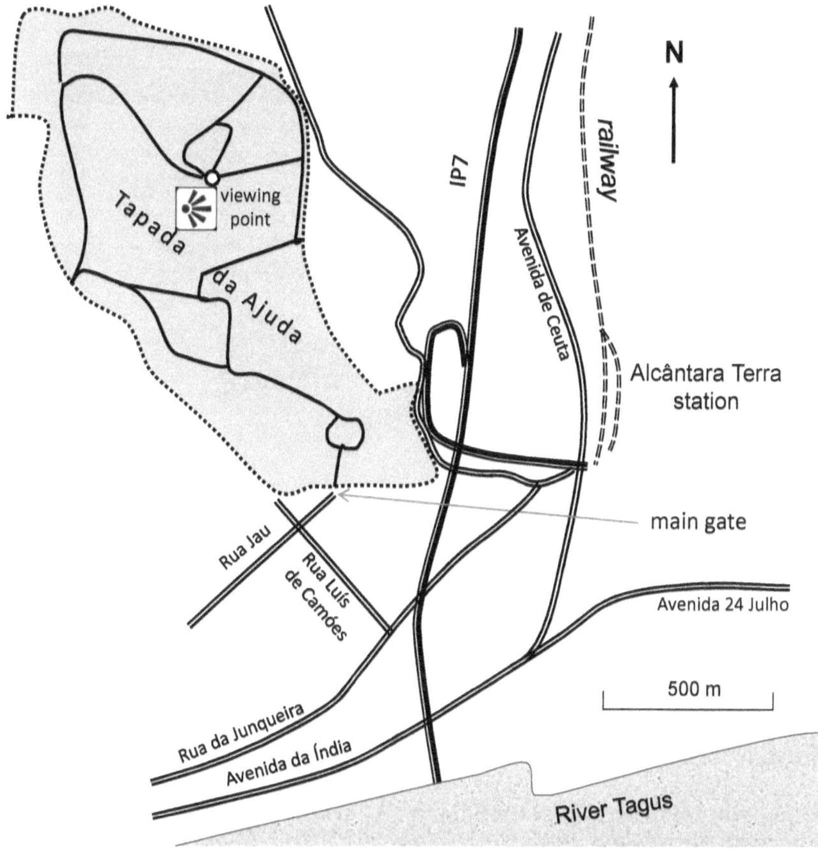

Just after passing the entrance, visitors can see the large building of the Instituto Superior de Agronomia (a university); in the surrounding fields, it is possible to see Red-legged Partridge, Kestrel, Barn Swallow, Zitting Cisticola and sometimes Linnet. The nearby trees usually hold Collared Dove and Greenfinch, whereas Chaffinch is regular in winter.

As the buildings are left behind, visitors enter the most densely wooded area of the Tapada. Typical birds here include Turtle Dove, Firecrest, Jay and several species of tits.

At the Tapada's highest point, there is a roundabout with a large Umbrella Pine in the middle. A few metres south of this roundabout, there is a viewing point, from where it is possible to see the city and the river. Swallows, Martins and Swifts can often be seen here.

Belém

The Belém area is very popular among tourists, mainly because of its famous monuments, which are part of the World Heritage List. Around here it is possible to find a few interesting birds.

Birds

Resident: Yellow-legged Gull, Black Redstart, Sardinian Warbler, Firecrest, Short-toed Treecreeper, Crested Myna, Spotless Starling

Non-breeding visitors: Cormorant, Sanderling, Common Sandpiper, Turnstone, Mediterranean Gull, Black-headed Gull, Lesser Black-backed Gull, Sandwich Tern, Meadow Pipit, European Starling

How to visit it

There are two main places of interest – the large garden called Praça do Império, just in front of the Jerónimos (Hieronymites) monastery and the area around Torre de Belém, slightly further west.

The Praça do Império is probably the best place in Lisbon to find the exotic Crested Myna. This bird, which is now widespread, can often be seen in the gardens and has been found breeding in the Hieronymites monastery. Other birds often seen in the gardens include Short-toed Treecreeper, Firecrest and Spotless Starling.

Not far from here, near the famous pastry factory 'Pastéis de Belém', lies the Botanical Garden (Jardim Botânico Tropical), which also holds several land birds. The exotic Senegal Parrot has been seen here.

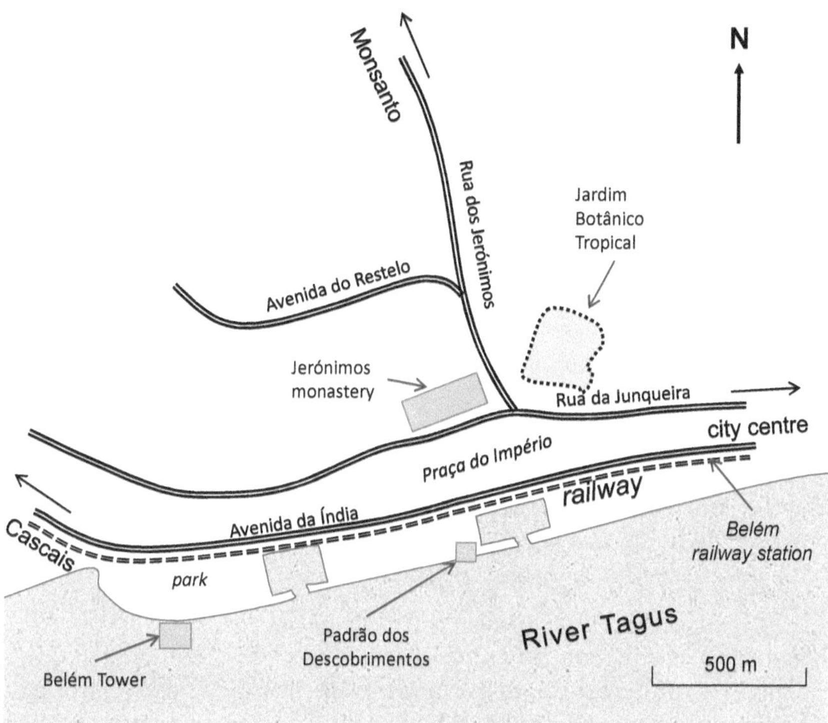

The shore of the river Tagus is formed by a long tilted wall, which is rather unsuitable for birds. However, during low tide, some muds and sands get exposed, especially around Torre de Belém (Belém Tower), and a few waders are often seen feeding alongside the wall, mainly Turnstones and Sanderlings. Gulls are usually frequent along the river, the most common species being Mediterranean, Black-headed, Lesser Black-backed and Yellow-legged (the latter can be seen year round and possibly breeds in the area). Cormorant is regular in autumn and winter, usually flying low over the water. Under adverse weather conditions, seabirds might enter the river – Gannets have been recorded here.

Parque Bensaúde

A rather small park in the north-western sector of the city. This location is especially noted as a regular site for the Senegal Parrot.

Birds

Resident: Woodpigeon, Ring-necked Parakeet, Blue-headed Parakeet, Senegal Parrot, Great Spotted Woodpecker, Black Redstart, Sardinian Warbler, Firecrest, Coal Tit, Short-toed Treecreeper, Jay, Spotless Starling, Serin

Breeding visitors: Turtle Dove, Pallid Swift, House Martin, Red-rumped Swallow

Non-breeding visitors: Chiffchaff, Pied Flycatcher, Chaffinch

How to visit it

Lies close to the Luz football stadium and can be reached by underground (Laranjeiras or Alto dos Moinhos). The park has two entrances, one on the east side and a smaller one on the north side.

This park is formed by large trees of various species, including a nice alley of maples. There is also a small vegetable garden.

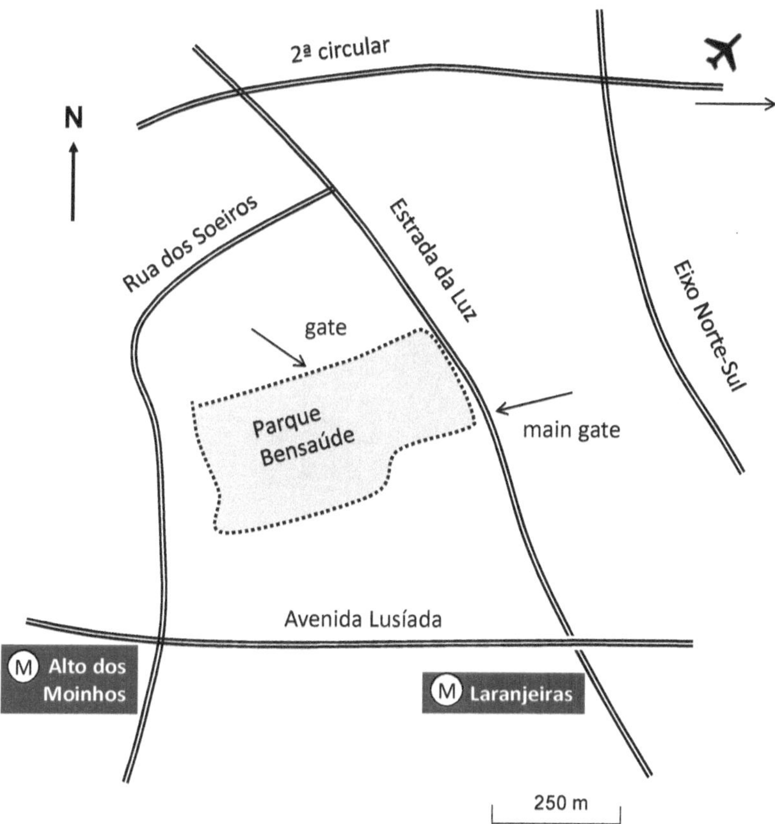

By entering through the main gate, visitors start walking uphill. A small vegetable garden appears on the right side and is worth inspecting, as it is often used by small birds, which get here to feed.

The upper (western) half of the park has some of the largest trees and it is here that the psittacids are usually found. The Senegal Parrot has been regularly recorded and it is possible that breeding takes place nearby. These birds are often perched on the large Maple or Eucalyptus trees. Maples have no leaves in winter and thus birds can be easier to spot at this time of year. Blue-headed and Ring-necked Parakeets are also recorded regularly and so it is actually possible to see the three exotic species during the same visit.

Apart from the psittacids, this park also holds a variety of songbirds. Some of them are resident, while others, such as the Pied Flycatcher, can be found on migration. The rare Yellow-browed Warbler has been recorded here on several occasions and other surprises may occur!

Jardim Calouste Gulbenkian

This is a pleasant garden with large trees and a small lake. It is a rather quiet place which is suitable for a small birdwatching break. It is the best place in Lisbon to see Moorhen.

Birds

Resident: Egyptian Goose (feral), Mallard (feral), Moorhen, Woodpigeon, Ring-necked Parakeet, White Wagtail, Wren, Blackbird, Blackcap, Coal Tit, Blue Tit, Short-toed Treecreeper, Spotless Starling, House Sparrow, Serin, Greenfinch

Breeding visitors: Common Swift, Pallid Swift, Barn Swallow

Non-breeding visitors: Lesser Black-backed Gull, Kingfisher

How to visit it

This place can only be visited on foot. There are several gates, with the main one on the north side and smaller ones on the eastern and western sides.

The main feature of this garden is the lake that lies in the middle, just behind the main building. Mallards and Egyptian Geese are usually around (but these birds are mainly feral). Moorhen can also be found here and it breeds regularly, taking advantage of the dense growth, which provides cover when there is too much disturbance. Kingfisher has been recorded outside the breeding season.

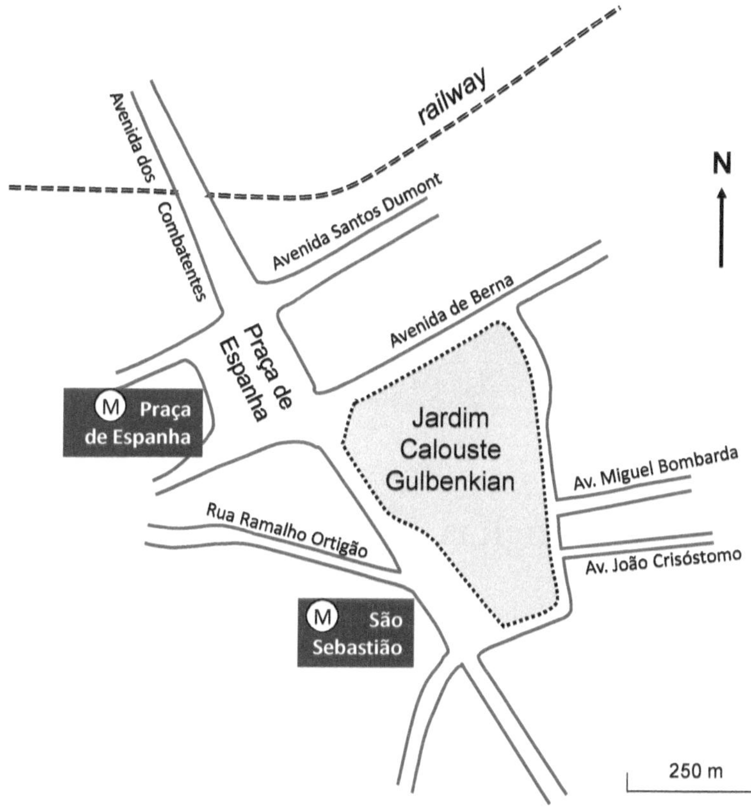

It is also worth inspecting the surrounding areas, which are covered with more or less dense vegetation. In the trees it is possible to see common garden birds such as Woodpigeon, Blackcap, Serin and Greenfinch. The exotic Ring-necked Parakeets are seen regularly at this place and are usually located by their noisy calls.

In the more open areas, covered with short grass, it is possible to see White Wagtail, Blackbird and the ubiquitous House Sparrow.

Quinta das Conchas

A medium-sized park (24 ha) in the northern part of the city. The lower sector is covered with lawn, while the rest is more densely wooded.

Birds

Resident: Egyptian Goose (feral), Woodpigeon, Ring-necked Parakeet, Blue-headed Parakeet, White Wagtail, Blackcap, Sardinian Warbler, Firecrest, Coal Tit, Short-toed Treecreeper, Jay, Spotless Starling, Serin

Breeding visitors: Pallid Swift, Barn Swallow, House Martin

Non-breeding visitors: Black-headed Gull, Song Thrush, Chaffinch

How to visit it

Lies close to the Alvalade XXI football stadium and is served by underground (Quinta das Conchas). There are several gates, but the main one is on the south side.

The park is actually formed by two sections: Quinta das Conchas on the southern half and Quinta dos Lilases on the northern half (the latter is much smaller). Each of these sections has a small lake, but these are rather unattractive for waterbirds – the only regular species are Egyptian Goose (introduced), Mallard and sometimes a few gulls.

The western (lower) part of the park is covered by a large lawn with a few scattered trees. Here it is possible to see Woodpigeon, White Wagtail, Blackbird and Spotless Starling. The large trees around here are often used as a perch by small flocks of Blue-headed Parakeets – this is probably one of the best places in the city to see this exotic parrot, which may already be breeding in the area. Ring-necked Parakeets are also common here. Chaffinch occurs in winter.

As visitors walk into the park, they enter its upper part, which has a small but dense woodland. Here it is possible to find Firecrest, Coal Tit, Short-toed Treecreeper and Jay, along with a few finches.

In summer the whole area is visited by Pallid Swifts and many hirundines (namely Barn Swallow and House Martin).

21

Parque da Bela Vista

A fairly large park on top of a hill in the eastern part of Lisbon. This park is one of the largest open areas within the city. It is formed by a mix of lawn and small patches of forest, mainly pine, olive and oak.

Birds

Resident: Woodpigeon, Ring-necked Parakeet, Hoopoe, Crested Lark, Black Redstart, Sardinian Warbler, Firecrest, Coal Tit, Short-toed Treecreeper, Spotless Starling, Serin

Breeding visitors: Common Swift, House Martin

Non-breeding visitors: Chaffinch, Meadow Pipit, European Starling

How to visit it

The main entrance lies on the eastern side. Cars are not allowed inside the park, but free parking is available just outside the gate.

Several paths run through the park and the best approach is probably to follow the outermost ones, in order to complete a large circle all around the park.

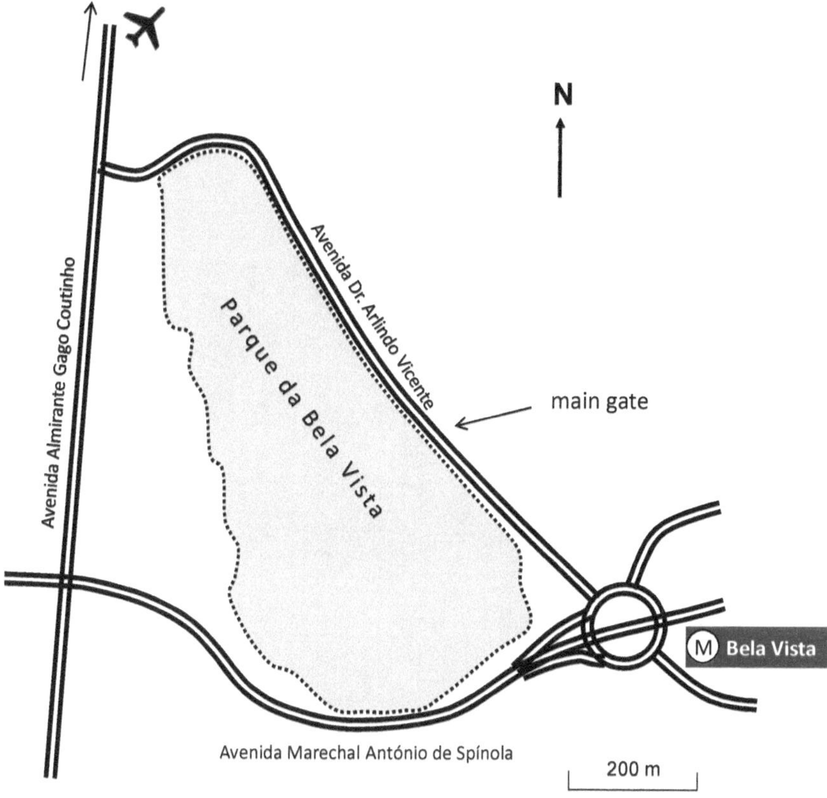

The more open areas, covered with lawn, have White Wagtail and Crested Lark, while Meadow Pipit is a winter visitor and Hoopoe is seen occasionally.

The pine woods are the best place to look for Firecrest, Coal Tit and Short-toed Treecreeper. The best patches of pine lie on the eastern and southern parts.

On the west side there is a small area of cork oak which is also worth exploring.

As to exotic parakeets, both Ring-necked and Blue-crowned Parakeet have been recorded, although the latter seems to be more common on the western half of town and is only occasionally recorded here.

This park is not often visited by birdwatchers, so the information available is quite scarce; it is possible that other species of interest occur here, especially during migration periods.

Matinha

This is a section of the Lisbon harbour and lies on the shore of the Tagus, very close to the estuary. During low tide, Matinha is a good place to look for waterbirds, especially waders.

Birds

Resident: Yellow-legged Gull, Black Redstart, Spotless Starling, House Sparrow, Serin

Non-breeding visitors: Cormorant, Little Egret, Grey Heron, Avocet, Ringed Plover, Kentish Plover, Sanderling, Dunlin, Common Sandpiper, Turnstone, Black-headed Gull, Mediterranean Gull, Lesser Black-backed Gull, Sandwich Tern

How to visit it

Lying on the shore of the Tagus, the Matinha area comprises a large section of estuarine muds and so this is one of the best places in town to look for waterbirds, namely herons, egrets, waders and gulls. It can be reached by car, but only if driving from south to north. So if coming from the north, get to the large roundabout near Poço do Bispo and then drive northwards for about 600 metres until an exit appears.

Follow it and look for a large metallic structure that lies at the end of a pier. Park near the pier and take a look around.

This location is more interesting in autumn and winter, especially during low tide. Gulls are usually plentiful, with Black-headed and Lesser Black-backed being the dominant species. Sometimes flocks of Mediterranean Gulls are also seen, even as early as July. Grey Herons are often present and occasionally Little Egrets turn up. More rarely, Flamingos put in appearance - in January 2009 there were six feeding in this place. Spoonbill has also been recorded here.

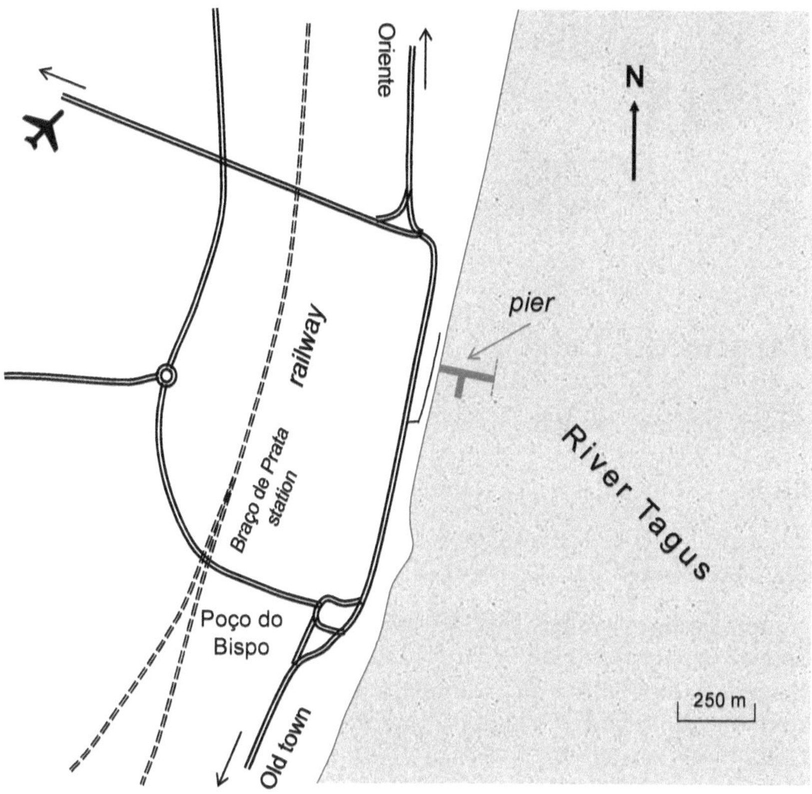

Outside the breeding season, it is possible to find small flocks of shorebirds. The usual species are Ringed Plover, Turnstone, Common Sandpiper and Sanderling, but other species turn up occasionally, including Avocet, Dunlin and Kentish Plover. This site is also noteworthy for its large roost of Cormorants. These birds like to perch on the metallic structure mentioned above – during the winter period, this roost can hold more than 100 individuals and in January 2009 a record 189 birds were counted here.

Parque do Tejo

A park on the shore of the river Tagus, very close to the estuarine area.

Birds

Resident: Mallard, Little Egret, Kestrel, Peregrine, Crested Lark, Cetti's Warbler, Zitting Cisticola, Spotless Starling, Serin, Common Waxbill

Non-breeding visitors: Teal, Cormorant, Cattle Egret, Grey Heron, Spoonbill, Greater Flamingo, Marsh Harrier, Avocet, Grey Plover, Ringed Plover, Little Stint, Dunlin, Black-tailed Godwit, Bar-tailed Godwit, Whimbrel, Common Sandpiper, Redshank, Mediterranean Gull, Black-headed Gull, Lesser Black-backed Gull, Sandwich Tern Meadow Pipit

How to visit it

The park lies at the north-eastern corner of the city, about 1 km north of the Oriente railway station and close to the large Vasco da Gama bridge. Free parking is available just beneath the bridge.

The park itself consists of lawns with a few trees. Several paths cross the park and the birds are usually tame.

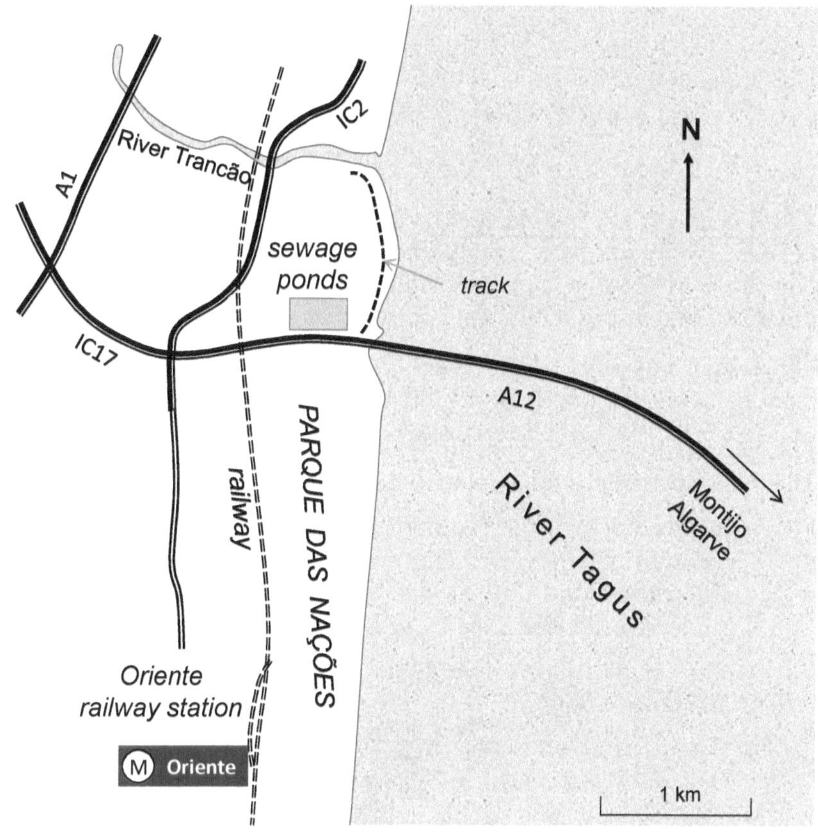

The most interesting part is the track that goes northwards close to the river Tagus. This track is about 1 km long and leads to the mouth of the Trancão, a smaller tributary. Along the way it is possible to see many waterbirds, namely waders, gulls, cormorants and sometimes flamingos.

Waterbirds are more numerous outside the breeding season, i.e. from August through April (in late spring and early summer the number of birds is very low).

It should also be emphasized that this sector is more interesting during low tide. When the tide is high, the muds are not exposed and most birds are feeding or roosting elsewhere.

The bridge itself should also be inspected: it is often used by one or two Peregrines – these birds use the large pylons as a perch and are sometimes seen flying around, hunting domestic pigeons. The sewage ponds just north of the bridge are also worth a look, as they sometimes attract gulls and waders.

Using public transport

For those without a car, it is still possible to get to all hotspots described here using public transport (either underground or bus).

The Lisbon bus network is called Carris; timetables and ticket prices can be checked online at http://www.carris.pt/. As to the underground ('Metro'), the website is http://www.metrolisboa.pt/.

The following list provides some tips about how to get to each hotspot.

- Monsanto – for the southern half, buses 723 and 729, leave at 'Montes Claros'; for the northern half, bus 711 stops at 'Monsanto' and 'Luneta dos Quartéis'; for Parque do Calhau, underground Blue Line to Jardim Zoológico

- Tapada da Ajuda – bus 760 or tram 18, leave at stop 'Pavilhão Desportivo Ajuda'

- Belém – buses 714, 727, 728, 729, 751 or tramway 15, leave at 'Mosteiro Jerónimos'; another possibility is to catch the train at Cais do Sodré and get out at Belém

- Parque Bensaúde – underground: Blue Line to Laranjeiras or Alto dos Moinhos; buses 701, 726 and 764, leave at the stop 'Bº São João'

- Jardim Calouste Gulbenkian: – underground: Red or Blue Line to São Sebastião or Blue Line to Praça de Espanha; buses 716, 726 and 756, leave at the stop 'Praça Espanha / Av. Berna'

- Quinta das Conchas – underground: Yellow Line to Quinta das Conchas; buses 717, 736 and 796, leave at the stop 'Av. Rainha Dona Leonor' or at 'Quinta das Conchas'

- Parque da Bela Vista – underground: Red Line to Bela Vista; buses 755 and 794, leave at the stop 'Parque da Bela Vista'

- Matinha – underground: Red Line to Oriente, then walk southwards; buses 728 and 781, leave at the stop 'Matinha'

- Parque do Tejo – underground: Red Line to Oriente, then walk northwards or take bus 26B or 708 to 'Rossio de Levante' or 'Passeio Tejo'

www.ingramcontent.com/pod-product-compliance
Lightning Source LLC
Chambersburg PA
CBHW031915270726
48655CB00003BA/1300